Jolliet and Marquette:

Explorers of the Mississippi River

Explorers of New Worlds

Jolliet and Marquette:

Explorers of the Mississippi River

Daniel E. Harmon

Chelsea House Publishers
Philadelphia

Prepared for Chelsea House Publishers by:
OTTN Publishing, Stockton, N.J.

CHELSEA HOUSE PUBLISHERS
Editor in Chief: Sally Cheney
Associate Editor in Chief: Kim Shinners
Production Manager: Pamela Loos
Art Director: Sara Davis
Director of Photography: Judy L. Hasday
Project Editors: LeeAnne Gelletly, Brian Baughan
Series Designer: Keith Trego

First Printing
1 3 5 7 9 8 6 4 2

Library of Congress Cataloging-in-Publication Data

Harmon, Daniel E.
    Jolliet and Marquette : explorers of the Mississippi
    River / Daniel E. Harmon.
        p. cm. – (Explorers of new worlds)
Includes bibliographical references and index.
ISBN 0-7910-6426-3 (hc) – ISBN 0-7910-6427-1 (pbk.)
1. Marquette, Jacques, 1637-1675–Juvenile literature.
2. Joliet, Louis, 1645-1700–Juvenile literature.
3. Mississippi River Valley–Discovery and exploration–
French–Juvenile literature. 4. Mississippi River Valley–
History–To 1803–Juvenile literature. 5. Explorers–
America–Biography–Juvenile literature. 6. Explorers–
France–Biography–Juvenile literature. [1. Marquette,
Jacques, 1637-1675. 2. Joliet, Louis, 1645-1700. 3. Explor-
ers. 4. Mississippi River–Discovery and exploration.]
I. Title. II. Series.

F352 .H27 2001
977'.01'0922–dc21
[B]   2001028275

Publisher's note: Louis Jolliet's name was spelled several
different ways during his lifetime: Jolliet, Joliet, and Jollyet.
The spelling has been standardized as Jolliet in this book,
because that is the variation most commonly used today.

Contents

Raging Waters

Louis Jolliet and Father Jacques Marquette listen to a Native American guide as they drift down the Mississippi River in birch bark canoes. In 1673, the French explorers led a small group of men down the river, hoping to find a westward route across North America to the Pacific Ocean.

I

rom far upstream they could hear it: a frightening yet awe-inspiring rush, as if two swift-flowing rivers were colliding. Were they approaching a stretch of perilous whitewater rapids? Perhaps a waterfall? The low, steady roar, growing louder moment by moment, undoubtedly was produced by tons of crashing, wild water. What should they do?

The **tumult** increased as Louis Jolliet, Father Jacques

Marquette, and their fellow explorers paddled their birch bark canoes down the western side of the Mississippi River. They began to see a great disturbance in the water ahead. The surface seemed to boil in a brownish tempest. Within it, large, heavy tree limbs—even whole, uprooted tree trunks—swirled and surged. There even were gruesome carcasses of drowned buffalo and other animals, some of which had been swept many miles through the prairies.

It seemed impossible for their frail canoes to enter this **maelstrom** without endangering their lives. But where could they turn? They braced themselves and plunged ahead, avoiding the large, heaving objects as best they could.

The explorers had come to the place where the great, muddy Missouri River joins the Mississippi. The men had arrived during the season when late spring thaws swell the Missouri to its highest levels. Melting snow in the high Rocky Mountains, far to the west, was sending flood **debris** and mud into the heart of North America. The amount of mud that

> **The Missouri River is an important watercourse in its own right. It flows some 3,000 miles before emptying into the Mississippi.**

poured in from the west was so great that from this point south, the Mississippi was a murky, almost undrinkable **watercourse**.

Jolliet and Marquette had never encountered such an event in their years of wilderness adventures. Marquette spoke of it in awe. "I have seen nothing more dreadful," he wrote. ". . . [L]arge and entire trees, branches, and floating islands were [flowing from the Missouri into the Mississippi] with such [force] that we could not without great danger risk passing through it. So great was the agitation that the water was very muddy, and could not become clear."

The scene may not seem very exciting to us in the 21st century. We witness powerful forces of human-made creations at work every day: blinding light displays, rockets and planes that shake nearby buildings and deafen us with their noise, dams that unleash water under incredibly high pressure to generate power, music played so loudly that it rattles windows several blocks away. Television news reports show us the wrath of nature, unleashed by tornadoes, floods, and uncontainable fires.

But to pioneers in North America 300 years ago, the sights beheld by Jolliet and Marquette were

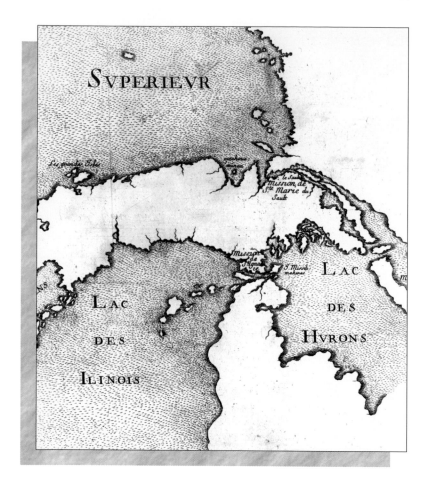

This detail from a French map of 1672, called the Jesuit Map, shows northern Michigan and portions of three of the Great Lakes: Superior, Michigan (identified here as Lac des Illinois) and Huron.

by no means ordinary. Shaggy beasts (buffalo), frightening creatures painted on massive river rocks (Indian art), fish so large they could capsize a canoe (channel catfish), a river so wide at places that it was hard to see across . . . such visions inspired awe when described around hearth fires and tavern tables. They had the same effect on people in 1673, the year of Jolliet and Marquette's expedition, that our most fantastic adventure movies have on viewers today.

The governor of the lands France had claimed in North America—called New France—had given the two hardy Frenchmen an important and daring assignment. Traveling southward from the Great Lakes, they were to put into the unexplored Mississippi River, the "great water" described by Native Americans. Jolliet and Marquette were ordered to follow it and see whether it led to the Pacific Ocean.

Today, this region of the American Midwest is the scene of busy cities and broad farmland. In the time of Jolliet and Marquette, it was the wild, mysterious western frontier. They did not know what forms of wildlife they would find, what natural wonders, what types of Native Americans. Every day brought sights and sounds never before experienced by Europeans. For them, it was a journey of great adventure . . . and uncertainty.

King Louis XIV ruled France from 1643 to 1715. He was dedicated to expanding France's power and lands, fighting several wars in Europe during his reign, and actively encouraging the exploration of North America.

France Claims a Frontier Empire

2

*I*n the late 17th century, King Louis XIV of France wanted to control North America. He wanted land in the New World because its countless miles of wilderness could satisfy the ambitions of adventurous French citizens. Also, the land he had in mind might be the critical link to the Pacific Ocean and the spice-rich Orient far beyond.

Remarkably, though France had claimed the land more than 100 years earlier, most of the king's large domain had never been seen by any French explorers. French Catholic **missionaries** and fur traders, or **voyageurs**, had only heard stories about it. The natives told of big lakes and a network of rivers teeming with fish, otter, and beaver. These waterways led for hundreds of miles through beautiful, untamed forests rich with wild game. The greatest of the rivers, it was said, led to an ocean.

In summer 1671, the king's agents invited the Native Americans living in the St. Lawrence River and Great Lakes region to a great *powwow*. It was held at the Sault Sainte Marie Catholic mission outpost. Located in modern-day Michigan, Sault Sainte Marie was an important center of frontier travel near the juncture of lakes Superior, Michigan, and Huron.

Indians of 14 nations gathered: Ottawa, Mohawk, Winnebago, Illinois, Ojibwa, Huron, Pottawattami, Shawnee, and others. For weeks, they feasted, played rough-and-tumble games, and tried to understand what the white men wanted. The French explained to the Indians as best they could that King Louis now was lord over all the region and was the Indians' king. The agents persuaded the chiefs to put their marks on a

New France was the name for French lands in North America during the 16th and 17th centuries. Today most of this territory is part of eastern Canada.

document agreeing to this arrangement. After this, the French considered themselves the official rulers of these lands.

The next big task for the French was to map out exactly what they had. They possessed crude maps, based on information reported to the authorities by trappers and traders. For the most part, these maps were not very accurate or complete. The few major rivers and streams that were shown had not been fully explored. Most important, almost nothing was known of the great Mississippi, the broad, mysterious waterway the Indians simply called the "great water." The French authorities wanted to know if it would provide a shortcut through North America to China and the lands of the Orient. If a route could be found through the continent, it could help the French develop a rich source of trade with the lands of the Far East.

> **The natives probably did not understand what they were being asked to do at the Sault Ste. Marie powwow. Most of the Indians did not understand the idea of one person "owning" the boundless territory they had roamed all their lives. And the idea that this new owner was to be a king they never had seen was strange indeed.**

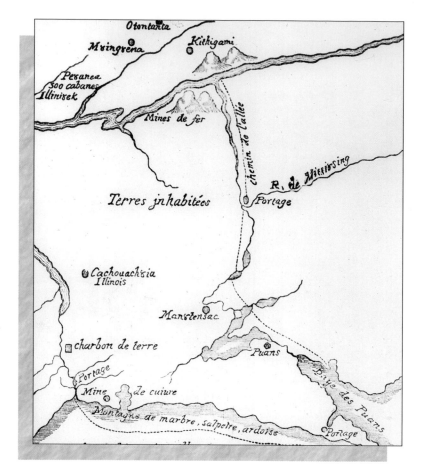

This map from a 17th century French book shows the area around the Great Lakes. The orientation is unlike maps of today, because the top of the map is South. The coast of Lake Michigan is located at the bottom, while the Mississippi River flows across the top.

In 1670, a Jesuit missionary named Father Claude Allouez had probed to the west of Lake Michigan, reaching the headwaters of the Wisconsin River. He was told that if a canoe headed downstream, in six days it would reach the "great water"—the wide river the Indians called the Mississippi. No Indian, they said, ever had journeyed to the end of it. Allouez, translating the way the natives pronounced the river's name, recorded it as "Messipi."

Another Jesuit missionary, Father Claude Dablon, was told by natives that the big river was very beautiful—and very different from the familiar St. Lawrence. It reportedly was much wider. For long stretches, Father Dablon wrote, it passed through "nothing but prairies, without trees or woods." Apparently, Spanish explorers had visited the mouth of the river and possibly dwelt there now. Word had spread through the Indian nations of men who looked like the French and who lived in a "house on the water"—obviously a ship.

If such a river ran through the very heart of the continent, then it was of enormous importance. Whichever country—France, Spain, or England—could conquer and rule this river valley would control the exploration and settlement of all North America.

The king in 1672 appointed Louis de Buade, Comte de Frontenac, to be the governor of New France. Frontenac was eager to bring unknown parts of the wilderness under French domain. He selected Louis Jolliet to find and explore this great river about which he'd heard so much.

Jolliet had actually been recommended for this task by Jean Talon, a powerful assistant to the governor of New France. Talon personally knew the leading fur traders of the territory. His first choice for the Mississippi expedition probably would have been Louis Jolliet's older brother Adrien. However, Adrien had never returned from an expedition to look for a copper mine near the Great Lakes in 1669. These expeditions were always dangerous— Adrien had probably been killed, although no one knows how, where, or when he died.

To Talon, Louis Jolliet was an easy second choice. Jolliet's ambition and knowledge of the lakes and rivers of the region suggested he would be the explorer most likely to succeed on such a quest. Talon's recommendation was seconded by Father Dablon, who held the important title of Jesuit Superior in New France. Dablon observed that Jolliet was courageous but not foolish. The hardy trader knew some of the Indian tribes and could communicate with them.

Talon was returning to France at about the time

*A group of Spanish soldiers led by Hernando de Soto
were the first Europeans to see the Mississippi River.
De Soto's party, which had landed in Florida in 1539,
arrived at the mighty river on May 9, 1541.*

Frontenac arrived. The new governor accepted
Talon's recommendation that Louis Jolliet lead the
expedition. Jolliet's mission was simple: to explore
the Mississippi and "discover the South Sea."

Not forgetting the French goal of converting the
Indians to Christianity, Frontenac ordered Father
Jacques Marquette, a Jesuit missionary, to go with

Jolliet. Marquette would be vital to the expedition because he could speak a number of Native American languages quite well. They were to travel with a few sturdy frontiersmen. Jolliet would be the leader.

Both Jolliet and Marquette were excited about the trip. Jolliet wanted to see this fabled river and the new trading opportunities it might have to offer. Marquette hoped to convert new Indian nations to the Catholic faith. He was especially eager to visit the Illinois Indians. Members of the Illinois tribe had asked him to teach the French language to one of their youths. Furthermore, Marquette wrote in his diary, they had urged him to "carry the word of God to their country."

The explorers knew it would be a difficult and dangerous journey. Outside the few towns, trading outposts, and Jesuit missions on the frontier, New France was a wild land. Not all the natives were friendly. The weather could be severe. If a man was hunting or trapping alone and was seriously injured, he would find no help for many miles. Death was almost certain.

The men would be traveling in birch bark canoes. The route was hazardous, the river's path changing with each major rainstorm.

Men in the wild lived by spearing or trapping fish (salmon, sturgeon, and pike), shooting large game (deer, elk, moose, and bear), and trapping small animals (beaver, fox, and otter). The fur of the animals was a valuable item that could be used to trade with Indians, sold at French trading posts, or **bartered** for supplies.

These rugged French woodsmen were called **coureurs de bois** (ku-ruhr-duh-bwah), or "runners of the woods." They often took Indian wives. They were an independent lot, relying on their skills for survival. Some of them were educated and honorable. Others were criminals who dealt treacherously with the Indians–and with each other. Many Jesuit missionaries thought that perhaps the *coureurs de bois*, their countrymen, needed spiritual conversion more than the Native Americans.

When it came to adventure and exploring new lands, though, New World missionaries and coureurs de bois shared a common interest. Father Marquette, like Jolliet, could not wait to see this mysterious river.

QUEBEC VEU DE L'EST

LAC S.T PIERRE

The Trader
and the
Priest

This 17th century French illustration shows the city of Quebec (top) and the St. Lawrence River. Louis Jolliet (inset) was a well-known woodsman and mapmaker who grew up in the French settlement in North America.

QUEBEC VEU DV NORD OUEST,

3

Who were these two men—the trader and the priest—to whom the governor gave such an important assignment?

Louis Jolliet was born in 1645 at Beauport, near the city of Quebec in New France. Situated on the great St. Lawrence River, Quebec was a major frontier post in North America. There, Jolliet went to a Jesuit school and studied to become a priest.

Jolliet was an excellent student, especially in math. He was also a talented musician, serving as an organist at the cathedral in Quebec. At 22, though, he decided he was not meant to be a clergyman. He left the Jesuit school in Quebec and sailed to France. There, he learned how to make maps. He focused on the mapping of oceans, lakes, and rivers. This special science is called *hydrography*.

After his mapmaking studies, Jolliet returned to the New World and turned his attention to the wild outdoors. He soon became an expert trapper and hunter. He did so well, in fact, that he established his own trading post at Sault Sainte Marie. He also earned a reputation as a careful map maker in New France.

French frontiersmen like Jolliet traded guns, black powder, knives, and trinkets to the Indians. In return, they received animal skins, which could be sold back in France. Beaver hides were especially in demand in Europe and brought high prices.

In 1669, when he was only 24 years old, Jolliet was sent by the governor to explore and map the Great Lakes. Based on this experience, Jolliet was a natural choice to lead the trip down the Mississippi four years later.

Jacques Marquette was born in Laon, capital of the Carolovingia province of France, in 1637. His hero as a young man was St. Francis Xavier, a missionary who had worked a century earlier spreading the gospel in the Far East. Marquette became a Roman Catholic priest, joining the Society of Jesuits at age 19. He studied and taught at Jesuit schools in France for the next 10 years. Then, in 1666, he volunteered to become a missionary to the Native Americans. The Society of Jesuits sent him to New France.

When Marquette first arrived in Quebec, he began his work by learning the languages of the native Ottawa and Huron Indians. Two years later, he helped establish the mission of St. Ignace at Sault Sainte Marie and began teaching the Ottawas about Christianity. Then Marquette moved on to other mission settlements on the Great Lakes.

Marquette was a very spiritual man who felt called to convert the people of the New World to Christianity. Marquette was not a stern, demanding preacher. He simply explained the message of the gospel. When natives converted, he allowed them to express their new faith in their unique tribal ways. For example, Indians liked to adorn crosses

St. Francis Xavier was an adventurer/explorer in his own right. In 1542, he sailed to India to work as a missionary, and in 1549 he became one of the first Europeans to visit Japan, where he spent two years preaching. He also wrote about the places he visited and people he met. Father Jacques Marquette (inset) also wanted to preach in lands unexplored by Europeans.

with ornaments. This practice would have upset Marquette's Catholic leaders back in France.

The Indians found Marquette especially likeable among all the missionaries. Many Native Americans held the missionaries—or "black robes," as the natives called them—in almost godlike awe. Father Marquette was special. According to one early 20th-century historian, John Fiske, "all who met him became aware of a heavenly presence."

Marquette also possessed literary talents as a writer of both poetry and prose. He carefully observed the people, plants, animals, and land features of the wilderness, and he remembered what he saw. Perhaps most important, in the eyes of Frontenac, Marquette was a brave, strong pioneer, able to face, as Fiske later wrote, "the fiercest extremes of hardship."

Jolliet and Marquette made ideal exploring partners because they were very much alike. Father Marquette, like his companion, faced the frontier without fear and possessed a spirit of adventure. He was far more interested in seeing what lay around the river's next bend than in collecting personal wealth. And he, like Jolliet, knew how to make friends with the natives.

The ability to establish friendships with Indians was extremely important. For many months, the men were to travel in unexplored, possibly hostile, surroundings. Unknown Native American tribes would be the only humans they encountered.

A Historic Mission

Since the early 17th century, when the French explorers Étienne Brulé and Samuel de Champlain reached the shores of the Great Lakes, adventurers in the New World had heard of the mighty river that the Indians called the "Great Water"— the Mississippi.

4

I n late 1672, Father Marquette was busy at the mission of St. Ignace, located at Michilimackinac (in present-day Michigan). This was in the Strait of Mackinac, which joins Lake Huron and Lake Michigan. He, like other missionaries, had heard the Native Americans of the area telling stories about the great Mississippi River. Marquette wished to see the river for himself. However, he believed that he would probably never get the chance.

Jolliet—"Monsieur Jollyet," as Marquette referred to him—arrived at the mission of St. Ignace in December 1672. He delivered a letter to Marquette from Father Dablon, his superior in Quebec. In the letter, Dablon told Marquette to prepare to go with Jolliet in the spring. His mission was to spread the word of Christ to Indians along the Mississippi River.

The priest and the trader were familiar with each other's work. They shared a mutual respect. They knew this would be a good partnership.

Father Marquette was eager to go on the trip. But traders and trappers like Jolliet, although rugged outdoorsmen who liked to live off the land, were also businessmen. How would Jolliet recover his lost time and trading profits? Superinten-

> Before receiving the order to accompany Jolliet, Father Marquette had wished to explore the Mississippi River on his own. Of course, missionaries had to stay at their missions. Marquette could not venture farther into the frontier unless his superiors ordered him to go. He thought his dream of visiting the Mississippi was unlikely ever to come to pass—until Jolliet arrived at the mission in December of 1672.

dent Talon had thought of this. He believed the government should grant trapping and trading privileges to Jolliet in return for his bold service. Among all the French trappers, only Jolliet and his partners should have the right to deal in furs from the Mississippi region.

Perhaps it did not occur to Talon that this special privilege would be practically worthless to Jolliet on his journey. Jolliet would be too busy finding his way and staying alive to think about stopping to trap wild animals and transport their furs all the way back to the settlements.

Undoubtedly, Jolliet realized this–but it hardly mattered. He wanted to explore the Mississippi not for profit, but for the adventure. This was a chance to satisfy his curiosity about a mighty river and an unknown land.

Jolliet and Marquette made their plans for the expedition and waited for warm weather. They asked the local Indians many questions, learning everything they could about the region. From this information, they sketched a map, hoping it would prove to be accurate.

The only foods the explorers planned to carry were smoked meat and dried Indian corn. Along the way, they would hunt fresh game and take fish from the rivers. They also made sure to pack one item that men of the woods did not always use: razors. For some reason, the Indians were known to show greater respect to Europeans who had beard-less faces like themselves—the missionaries, for example. Rough trappers who never bothered to shave often were scorned and abused by the natives. It was very important that Marquette and Jolliet make friends with the Indian nations they would meet along the Mississippi. The small task of shaving might prove to be of great value.

It seemed to the impatient explorers that the spring thaws would never come. Cold weather clung to the lakes after the normal winter season was over. The men were prepared to leave long before the frozen waters warmed and the ice began to loosen. They could not wait to be on their way.

Finally, the ice melted enough to permit travel. After a prayer for blessings on their journey, Jolliet and Marquette set out by birch bark canoe from St. Ignace on May 17, 1673. They had five companions: Pierre Largilier, Pierre Moreau, Jean Plattier, Pierre Porteret, and Jacques Tiberge. Most of these men were Jolliet's business partners. All were strong,

Father Marquette preaches to a group of Native Americans while the exploring party is stopped along the Mississippi River. The primary goal of missionaries like Marquette was to expose the natives to Christianity, and to try to convert them to the Catholic religion that the French followed.

seasoned frontiersmen who knew how to survive in difficult conditions.

The group skirted the northern coast of Lake Michigan and soon entered Green Bay. Marquette recorded its name in French as "Bay des Puants," which means "Bay of Stinking Waters." Green Bay is a very large, nearly enclosed body of water on northwestern Lake Michigan. Today the town by that name is a major city in the state of Wisconsin.

The party paddled all the way down the long bay. Each day, the explorers set out early in the morning and paddled until almost dark. It was hard, endless labor, but they hardly minded. They were so thrilled by the adventure that the wearisome hours seemed to pass quickly.

From the beginning, friendly Menomini natives begged them not to venture down the "big river" to where the sun burned exceedingly hot. Marquette wrote that the Menomini warned the Frenchmen about violent tribes to the south who would attack strangers and "break their heads without any cause. . . . They also said that the great river was very dangerous, when one does not know the difficult places; that it was full of horrible monsters, which devoured men and canoes together."

The Frenchmen were not deterred. They entered the Fox River at the lower end of Green Bay. To travel generally southward, they had to fight against the current of the Fox. "[The River] becomes very difficult of passage," Marquette wrote, "on account of both the currents and the sharp rocks, which cut the canoes and the feet of those who are obliged to drag them."

Yet the land around them was interesting and beautiful. At this time of year migrating birds were returning from their southern winter vacations. Wild rice grew along the banks and down into the river itself. The birds loved this grain, which was an important part of the local Indians' daily diet. Historian John Bakeless has estimated that "one small lake could produce enough [wild rice] to feed two thousand people."

Father Marquette was quite interested in these "wild oats," as he called them. He also described certain herbs that were valued by the Indians for various purposes. For example, he mentioned a type of root that, when chewed, was supposed to drive away poisonous snakes.

One day, the men arrived at a point where they needed to cross land to reach another river that would take them farther south. No French explorer had ever traveled past this point.

They took their canoes out of the Fox. With the help of two Miami Indians, they **portaged** the vessels and supplies through more than a mile–2,700 paces, by Father Marquette's count—of wet wilderness to the Wisconsin River. There, they put in their birch bark canoes and continued west-southwest.

The Wisconsin, they found, was wide, with sandy **shoals** and vine-covered islands. It was an excellent river for traveling by lightweight canoe. Just as important, wild game was plentiful there. The men were able to eat fresh meat practically every day. In almost every way, their passage down the Wisconsin was the most pleasurable part of their entire expedition.

It was now June. The approaching summer was particularly warm as they gradually made their way southwestward. Fog sometimes hung over the river in the morning as they began their day of travel. It created a mystical, gray setting for the new woodland they were gliding past with each rhythmic stroke of their paddles.

After navigating through the shoals for about a week, they came to the river's mouth and saw before them the Mississippi—the river they had come to explore.

To the two explorers' surprise, the Mississippi was not the awesome, broad waterway they had expected—not here, at any rate. At its headwaters, the Mississippi seems little different from shorter, less powerful rivers. But right away they found it to be unusually deep, about 60 feet.

They had completed their approach to the mighty watercourse. Now their mission would begin in earnest. "[W]e safely entered [the Mississippi] on the 17th of June," Marquette wrote, "with a joy that I cannot express."

The Great Mississippi

A fanciful painting of Jolliet and Marquette in canoes paddled by brightly dressed Indians. As they made their way down the river, the French explorers saw many strange and wonderous things.

5

A s the explorers paddled down the Mississippi day after day, they realized something surprising—and disappointing. The river flowed generally south, not west as the French had hoped. If it flowed into a great body of water as the Indians claimed, then that ocean must be the Gulf of Mexico, not the Pacific.

For about two weeks, they glided down the western bank of the river. They were curious about the absence of any Native American hunting parties or villages along the shore. Then, possibly near what is now Peoria, Illinois, they found native footprints leading from the riverbank into the prairie. Jolliet and Marquette stopped and followed the tracks for some seven miles. When they saw an Indian village in the distance, they silently crawled toward it. They got so close they could hear the villagers talking.

To announce their presence, the Frenchmen stood up and shouted as loudly as they could. They believed this would let the Indians know they had come in peace, not as wily attackers. Although the natives were startled and defensive at first, they quickly realized the two men were not enemies.

Inhaling Indian tobacco was not a pleasant experience for the Europeans, but they endured it. They knew that to refuse would be an act of disrespect, and the Indians might become angry.

Marquette spoke several Indian languages, so he was able to communicate with these Native Americans, who turned out to be quite friendly. They fed their visitors and gave them *calumets*, or peace pipes, to smoke. They gave the Frenchmen a special calumet to take with them. It would protect

*Marquette holds aloft a calumet, showing a group of
Native Americans that the French came in peace.*

them, the natives said, and would show other tribes
that the white visitors had been accepted. The chief
of the tribe also gave them a much more important
gift. He presented Jolliet with a small boy, his own
son, to accompany them as a sign of lasting friend-
ship. Jolliet politely tried to persuade the chief to let
the boy remain behind with his own people, but the
Indian leader insisted. He also advised them to stay,
warning that hostile tribes lived downriver.

Jolliet and Marquette were not discouraged. They had known they might meet natives who would not be happy to see them. Their mission was to explore the river, and they were determined to proceed. They took safety measures, though, from then on. When they stopped for the night, they posted a guard on shore and slept in canoes anchored farther out in the water. This would make it harder for hostile natives to mount an attack in the darkness.

Marquette described in his journal some of the wildlife they saw. He called the buffalo *pisikious,* or "wild cattle." These animals were unknown to the travelers. Marquette wrote:

> The head is very large; the forehead is flat and a foot and a half wide between the horns. . . . Under the neck they have a sort of large dewlap, which hangs down; and on the back is a rather high hump. The whole of the head, the neck, and a portion of the shoulders are covered with a thick mane like that of horses; it forms a crest a foot long, which makes them hideous, and, falling over their eyes, prevents them from seeing what is before them. The remainder of the body is covered with a heavy coat of curly hair, almost like that of our sheep, but much stronger and thicker. It falls off in summer, and the skin becomes as soft as velvet. . . . The flesh and the fat of the pisikious are excellent, and constitute the best dish at feasts.

The buffalo, he reported, roamed the prairies in herds—some containing as many as 400 animals.

The Frenchmen were afraid to get too close to the buffalo they saw while traveling down the Mississippi. "When attacked, they take a man with their horns, if they can, lift him up, and then dash him on the ground, trample on him, and kill him," Marquette wrote.

Later pioneers would report much larger herds of buffalo farther west. But to Jolliet and Marquette, who were seeing these animals for the first time, even a small group was exciting. Their descriptions of buffalo would cause quite a stir back in Quebec and, eventually, in the French king's court.

Occasionally, Marquette wrote, they encountered "monstrous fish, one of which struck our canoe with such violence that I thought that it was a great tree, about to break the canoe to pieces." This may have been either a channel catfish or a sturgeon, both of which can grow very large. The explorers estimated some of the fish they saw weighed as much as 150 pounds.

Another "monster" Marquette saw in the river seemed very odd. It had "the head of a tiger, a sharp nose like that of a wildcat, with whiskers and straight, erect ears; the head was gray and the neck quite black." This was probably a cougar or some other wildcat swimming in the current.

Just as strange and unnerving, but in a different way, were the "monsters" they saw painted on a large rock on the river's high, steep eastern shore. The images were so frightful, Marquette said, that even "the boldest Indian dare not gaze long" at them. He described them in his journal: "They are as large as a calf, with horns on the head like a deer, a fearful look, red eyes, bearded like a tiger, the face somewhat like a man's, the body covered with scales, and the tail so long that it twice makes the turn of the body, passing over the head and down between the legs, and ending at last in a fish's tail. Green, red, and a kind of black, are the colors employed."

Native rock paintings like this were common around the upper Mississippi River and Great Lakes. They often told stories about events that supposedly happened among the Indians many years before. In this case, the painting recalled the tale of a fabled monster, part bird and part animal or fish, that was said to have killed many Indians until a group of bold warriors finally slew it.

Marquette found it hard to believe that this art could be the creation of Indians. French master painters would have found the work difficult to imitate, he said. And the rock was situated so high that it must have been very hard for the painter—or painters—to work there.

In many cases, even the wildest myths are based on a kernel of truth. Interestingly, 300 years after Jolliet and Marquette's journey, a cave in the cliffs was found to contain a mass of human bones. Perhaps the fantastic monster of the legend—or at least some gigantic bear or other beast—actually existed and terrorized the Indian villages.

Near the site of the modern-day city of St. Louis, Missouri, the voyagers passed the turbulent mouth of the Missouri river. Natives called the river the Pekistanoui—"Big Muddy." The priest wondered whether it might bring them near the Pacific Ocean, if they followed it upstream. Someday, he hoped, he would have time to explore it and find out.

Expanded by the Missouri's dirty waters, the Mississippi River now was even more powerful and impressive than before. At places the explorers saw dangerous, foaming whirlpools, much wider than the length of their canoes, with logs and limbs circling endlessly inside them. Frequently along the river they had to dodge snags—uprooted trees that temporarily caught on the river bottom and protruded a foot or so above the surface. Some of the snags lay just below the surface, able to rip open or capsize a canoe whose crew did not see the danger in time to swerve away.

As they continued southward, the Frenchmen found the summer heat almost unbearable. They also were plagued by mosquitoes. The Indians, Marquette recorded, escaped the mosquitoes by sleeping over a smouldering fire on platforms with floors of loose-fitted poles. The smoke from the fire underneath crept between the poles, keeping the mosquitoes away.

It seems odd that the Indians chose to endure the heat and smoke themselves. Apparently, to them, the heat was not as bad as the mosquitoes!

Farther and farther south the Frenchmen paddled. They were seeing birds, animals, and trees not common to their northern homeland. The *canebrakes* below the mouth of the Ohio River were especially interesting. These were marshy areas heavily overgrown with tall woody grasses and hollow reeds. Jolliet and Marquette found them to be teeming with colorful and strange animals and birds, like the brightly colored Carolina parakeet.

It was a fascinating voyage. But the explorers were beginning to wonder . . . just how far should they go?

Time to Turn Back

After two months on the river, Jolliet and Marquette decided to turn back to New France. They were afraid that they would encounter hostile Indians and Spaniards if they continued south; also, they believed they had already learned what they had journeyed to find.

6

he expedition followed the Mississippi south to a place where another large waterway—the Arkansas River—merged into it. At this junction, the men found more friendly Native Americans. But these people told the Frenchmen that other Indians resented the Europeans' presence. That information, coupled with rumors that hostile Spaniards lived downriver, made Jolliet and Marquette think perhaps it was time to turn back.

It was hard to decide. On the one hand, they knew from what the Indians told them that the Gulf of Mexico was near—no more than a few days away. However, there was little doubt what would happen if the Spaniards captured them. At best, they would be held captive, perhaps for years. They might be killed. What good would their detailed description of the Mississippi River be if they could not return to King Louis and make their report?

The threat was not only from the Spaniards, but from the Native Americans. Some of the Indian tribes on the lower Mississippi had allied themselves with the Spanish. The Spaniards had given them guns and taught them how to shoot. If it came to a fight, the small band of French explorers would have little chance of escaping, much less winning.

Another problem that was getting worse as they paddled southward was communication. Father Marquette could speak many Indian languages, but they were all of the northern tribes. Here, the Native American spoke in very different tongues that he could not understand. The French could obtain only basic information from the Native Americans through sign language and a few words. The language barrier was frustrating as they attempted to ask questions that would draw details about the land and people of the lower Mississippi.

Jolliet and Marquette discussed the problem. They decided they had already learned what they had been sent to find out: the Mississippi River flowed southward into the gulf, not westward into the Pacific.

On July 17, two months after they had left St. Ignace, they pointed their canoes northward into the current. Traveling against the river's powerful flow was not easy. Sleeping as they did in their anchored canoes at night provided only fitful rest. Mosquitoes plagued them. The heat this far down-river made the upstream paddling more agonizing. Father Marquette came down with a fever. But day by toilsome day, they made their way homeward.

The men took a different route from their southerly course. When they came to the mouth of the Illinois River, they paddled up that waterway toward the Great Lakes. It proved to be an enchant-ing relief from their labors on the Mississippi.

The surface of the Illinois was smooth, and its current was not nearly as strong as that of the larger river. Marquette and Jolliet were both quite impressed by the Illinois. Its soil and forests were

IN · HONOR · OF
LOUIS·JOLLIET·&·PÈRE·JACQUES·MARQUETTE

This plaque commemorating the journey of Jolliet and Marquette is located on a bridge in Chicago.

especially rich. They saw many kinds of wildlife. Jolliet began to think of someday returning to this territory to live, perhaps to build a farm and trading post.

From the headwaters of the Illinois, kind natives showed them where to portage the short distance to the Chicago River, which carried them to Lake Michigan. It occurred to Jolliet that a canal could be dug between the Illinois and Chicago rivers. Then a ship would be able to pass all the way from the Great Lakes to the Gulf of Mexico!

Jolliet and Marquette reached Green Bay in late September. They had traveled more than 2,500 miles, round-trip. Their party had navigated down the Mississippi to within several hundred miles of the Gulf of Mexico—the first Europeans to explore the river that far south.

Jolliet had not had time to make careful notes and maps along the way. He spent the winter at Sault Sainte Marie, writing his account of the expedition. He also did some trapping, knowing he could sell the animal pelts in Quebec to help cover some of the cost of his trip. In the spring, he set out for Quebec by canoe.

As he paddled homeward along the St. Lawrence River, his canoe flipped in the dangerous Lachine Rapids near modern-day Montreal. His precious papers were lost; he would have to try to reconstruct his maps from memory later.

The lost documents were the least of his concerns. Several of his companions and the Indian chief's young son whom he had brought back from the Mississippi drowned in the rapids. Luckily, Jolliet was not seriously injured, although he was in the chilly water for four hours.

Father Marquette, meanwhile, stayed at the Jesuit mission of St. Francis Xavier at the lower end of Green Bay. His health was failing badly, but he believed he still had work to do among the Indians.

Successful
Mission,
Sad Ending

René-Robert Cavelier, Sieur de La Salle, claims the Mississippi River valley for France. Nine years after Jolliet and Marquette explored the upper Mississippi, La Salle became the first European to follow the mighty river to its mouth in the Gulf of Mexico.

7

For the first time, Europeans had accurately charted the upper reaches of the Mississippi River. Much remained to be learned—and the lower Mississippi had to be navigated. In April 1682, René-Robert Cavelier, Sieur de La Salle, became the first European to travel the river all the way to the Gulf of Mexico. But thanks to Jolliet and Marquette, the French already knew that the Mississippi led not to the Pacific, but to the southern gulf.

Unfortunately, there was a negative consequence of Jolliet and Marquette's historic journey. The long trip down the Mississippi had ruined Father Marquette's health. He settled down for the winter to recover at the mission of St. Francis Xavier on Green Bay. There he wrote his narrative of the epic voyage. The next year, 1674, he believed he was well enough to go back into the wilds to preach to the Kaskaskia Indians in what is today Illinois.

It was autumn when he left the mission at Green Bay with two assistants. The weather was hostile. Thunderstorms were followed by snow. Fierce headwinds stalled their progress by canoe, sometimes for days on end. Wild game was hard to find, and Marquette became dreadfully sick once more.

The hard life of an explorer had taken a lasting toll on Marquette's body. The beating he took from the weather during this journey made him very weak. After spending the winter in a hastily built cabin near the present-day city of Chicago, Marquette made his way to the waiting Kaskaskia people, who regarded him almost as an angel.

Preaching was difficult, but Marquette did his best. The feeble priest held Easter Mass for several thousand spellbound Indians. Afterward, he told

Just two years after returning from the voyage down the Mississippi, Father Marquette died while returning to the mission he had founded on Lake Michigan.

them he needed to return by canoe to the mission on Lake Michigan and try once more to recover his health.

He never made it back. En route, realizing his time had come, he told his companions to take him ashore. He wrote a letter to his Jesuit brothers, confessing his sins. He told those with him that he would remember them in heaven. Soon afterward, he died peacefully with his eyes open as they held a *crucifix* before his face.

It was spring 1675, just two years after he and Jolliet had set out to explore the Mississippi. Father Marquette was only 38 years old.

Marquette's diaries provide important details of the history of the upper Mississippi and the Great Lakes. They contain not only careful descriptions and personal observations, but important maps of the region.

Jolliet's records also were useful–although he had to recreate them after his original papers were lost in the canoe accident. The successful explorer returned home to a less-than-enthusiastic welcome. Jolliet faced criticism and lawsuits–including a claim filed by his brother-in-law–because he did not return to Quebec with bundles of valuable furs to pay his partners and family. For a brief time, he was left in poverty. In the aftermath of the canoe wreck, he wrote, "all I saved is my life."

Soon, though, the governor of New France gave Jolliet the island of Anticosti in the Gulf of St. Lawrence as a reward for his explorations. He became a successful trader once again.

In 1675, Jolliet was married in Quebec. Later, he explored the Atlantic coast of New France and the extensive Hudson Bay in north-central Canada.

Some of these travels were spy missions, during which he obtained information about the New World activities of England, France's ancient enemy.

Jolliet was appointed the king's official mapper of oceans and rivers. The Jesuits in Quebec hired him to teach navigation skills at their college. He became a wealthy trader, but he lost his fortune when the English invaded Anticosti Island. They destroyed his trading post and held his family captive for some time. Jolliet died in 1700; the circumstances of his passing are not known.

One of the most remarkable things about Louis Jolliet and Father Jacques Marquette is that they were respected by everyone. They got along very well together—unlike some explorers, who dealt with mutiny or attacks by their own companions. They established friendly relations with most of the Indian tribes they met. And they were treated well by those in political power in Quebec and France.

In all the centuries of exploration, perhaps two more agreeable partners never embarked into the wilderness together. They discovered much about the land and people of the Mississippi River valley, making the efforts of later explorers like La Salle much easier.

Chronology

1637 Jacques Marquette is born in Laon, France, on June 1.

1645 Louis Jolliet is born near Quebec City, New France, in September.

1666 Marquette is sent to work with the Indians in New France.

1672 On December 8, Jolliet arrives in Michilimackinac on the Great Lakes to join Father Marquette and begin preparing for their spring expedition.

1673 Jolliet and Marquette with five others depart Michilimackinac to explore the Mississippi River on May 17; the explorers come to the mouth of the Wisconsin River and enter the upper Mississippi on June 17; on July 17, near the mouth of the Arkansas River and several hundred miles from the mouth of the Mississippi, the explorers turn back, arriving in Green Bay in late September.

1675 On May 8, Father Marquette dies of an intestinal disorder while returning from a wilderness missionary journey.

1682 René-Robert Cavelier, Sieur de La Salle, reaches the Gulf of Mexico via the Mississippi River on April 9.

1700 Louis Jolliet dies in unknown circumstances, apparently on or near the St. Lawrence River.

barter–to trade valuable items, rather than buying and selling them with money.

calumet–a beautifully decorated peace pipe used by Indians in special ceremonies.

canebrake–an area in which tall, woody grasses or reeds grow.

coureurs de bois–a name for frontier-era French woodsmen.

crucifix–a representation of Jesus Christ on the cross.

debris–waste or trash, usually broken remains.

hydrography–the art or science of mapping and charting bodies of water.

maelstrom–an area of swirling violence on the surface of water.

missionary–a person who tries to convert other people to his or her religion.

portage–to carry a boat and/or supplies overland from one river to another, or from one area of a river to another.

powwow–a gathering of Native Americans for celebrating or negotiating.

shoal–a place in a river, lake, or ocean where sandbars rise to just beneath the surface of the water.

tumult–a great noise or commotion.

voyageur–a type of French frontiersmen who served as a wilderness guide and transporter of furs and supplies between the interior of North America and its settlements.

watercourse–a channel, either natural or artificial, through which water flows.

Further Reading

Bakeless, John. *The Eyes of Discovery.* Philadelphia: J.B. Lippincott Company, 1950.

Cumming, W.P., et al. *The Exploration of North America, 1630-1776.* New York: G. P. Putnam's Sons, 1974.

Eifert, Virginia S. *Louis Jolliet: Explorer of Rivers.* New York: Dodd, Mead & Company, 1962.

Edmonds, Walter D. *The Musket and the Cross.* Boston: Little, Brown and Company, 1968.

Fiske, John. *New France and New England.* Cambridge, Mass.: The Riverside Press, 1902.

Harmon, Daniel E. *La Salle and the Exploration of the Mississippi.* Philadelphia: Chelsea House, 2001.

Hatcher, Harlan. *The Great Lakes.* London: Oxford University Press, 1944.

Syme, Ronald. *Voyagers on the Mississippi: Marquette and Joliet.* New York: William Morrow and Company, 1974.

Picture Credits

DANIEL E. HARMON is associate editor of *Sandlapper: The Magazine of South Carolina* and editor of *The Lawyer's PC*, a national computer newsletter. He has written more than 20 nonfiction books on history, humor, and other topics, including *La Salle and the Exploration of the Mississippi* for Chelsea House's EXPLORERS OF NEW WORLDS series. He lives in Spartanburg, South Carolina.